LIVING WITH LESS
AN UNEXPECTED KEY TO HAPPINESS

JOSHUA BECKER

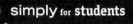

Living With Less
An Unexpected Key To Happiness

© 2012 Joshua Becker

group.com
simplyyouthministry.com

Credits
Author: Joshua Becker
Executive Developer: Nadim Najm
Chief Creative Officer: Joani Schultz
Editor: Rob Cunningham
Art Director and Production: Veronica Preston

ISBN 978-0-7644-8660-9

10 9 8 7 6 5 4 3 2 1   20 19 18 17 16 15 14 13 12

Printed in the United States of America.

Joshua Becker is about to introduce you to a different way of thinking: Your life is too valuable to waste it chasing stuff. The idea isn't one you'll hear very often in our culture, but it is one that could change your life and even more importantly change your heart.

Joshua Griffin
High School Pastor
Saddleback Church

Joshua has created a resource that is challenging and thought-provoking! If students (or even adults) are willing to engage with it, the ideas can transform how they look at "stuff" ...starting today.

Scott Rubin
Junior High Pastor
Willow Creek Community Church

Joshua's work in this book serves as a voice calling parents and students to live for more than just "stuff." Living With Less *is a reminder that there is something else...something better.*

Mike Burns
Pastor of Family Development
The Chapel, Getzville, New York

Today's teenagers are pitched this and that all day long, but rarely are they exposed to a truly compelling and contemporary way of living that is somehow both counterintuitive and so obviously biblical.

Mark Oestreicher
Partner
The Youth Cartel

I love to promote simple living, but it's become trendy— so trendy, in fact, that it's easy to write it off as just another lifestyle fad. But it's so much more than a fad; it's a way of life prescribed to all Jesus-followers. I wish I was encouraged more to pursue a life free from stuff when I was a teenager. In other words, I wish I'd had this book. Joshua challenges teens to free their hearts from the pursuit of stuff, and his words are gold.

Tsh Oxenreider
Founder and Editor of SimpleLivingMedia.com

There are times in our lives when powerful truths hit us straight on with force. Joshua's book was one of those times for me. If you need a facelift on your life this is a must read.

Nate Parks
Executive Director
Camp Berea, New Hampshire

Living With Less has the potential to change the next generation, to show them the futility of chasing "stuff" and make them step back and really evaluate the decisions they make in light of Christ's teachings. In a world where the pursuit of happiness has become synonymous with the pursuit of stuff, it's time to turn the tide and rediscover lives of simplicity and freedom.

Mandi Ehman
Founder & Editor
Life Your Way (life.yourway.net)

There's a lot to look forward to in life. Joshua is right on when he encourages readers to pass on consumerism and live for Jesus. No need to worry about returns or next season's fashion. Living for Jesus means no regrets.

Dave Bruno
Author of *The 100-Thing Challenge*

This book invites teens to practice minimalism in response to God's life-giving invitation to live with less. Joshua Becker shares his story and leads by example while offering practical ways to discover what is most important in life.

Courtney Carver
Author of *Be More With Less*

Minimalism is often dismissed as a trendy lifestyle for 20-somethings without the burdens of married life, children, or responsibilities. Joshua Becker debunks this misconception by telling his story of his suburban family of four's journey toward simpler lives, embracing minimalism and enjoying the benefits of living more intentionally.

Joshua Field Millburn
Blogger at theminimalists.com

DEDICATION

special thanks to my wife, Kimberly.
dedicated to my beautiful children, Salem
and Alexa.

these words originated in the grace of God...
by a life invested into by countless godly men
and women...

and are written for an audience destined to
find full life in Christ alone.

TABLE OF CONTENTS

Introduction i

PART 1: JESUS' STORY 1

Chapter 1: Jesus and the Offer of
Abundant Life 3

Chapter 2: Jesus and Possessions 17

PART 2: MY STORY 27

Chapter 3: A Pretty Typical Story of
Too Much Stuff..29

Chapter 4: An Introduction to a New
Way of Life...37

PART 3: YOUR STORY 43

Chapter 5: Our Actions Follow Our Heart.....45

Chapter 6: The Life-Changing Benefits
of Owning Less 53

Chapter 7: The Heart Impact of
Choosing Less...69

Chapter 8: A Word to the Skeptics..............75

PART 4: THE INTERSECTION OF YOUR STORY AND JESUS' STORY 79

Chapter 9: Maybe Jesus Has Been
Right All Along...81

Chapter 10: Making Jesus' Story Yours........89

Chapter 11: Your Life Is Too Valuable
to Spend Chasing Possessions..................101

ENDNOTES.................................... 105

INTRODUCTION

Nobody really believes it...

Nobody really believes it. Nobody really believes possessions equal joy. In fact, if specifically asked the question, nobody in their right mind would ever say the secret to a joyful, meaningful life is to own a lot of stuff. Deep down in their heart, nobody really thinks it's true. Yet almost all of us live like it is.

From the moment we are born, we are told to pursue more. Advertisements from every television, radio, newspaper, magazine, billboard, and website scream to us on a daily basis that more is better. As a result, we spend countless hours comparing our things to the person next to us. We measure our family's success in life by the size of our home. And we end up looking for jobs that pay enough money so we can spend our adult lives purchasing the biggest homes, fanciest cars, trendiest fashions, most popular toys, and coolest technologies.

But we all know it's not true. We all know happiness cannot be bought at a department store. More is not necessarily better. We've just been told the lie so many times we begin to believe it...without even noticing.

Consider some of these statistics:

- The average American cardholder carries 3.7 credit cards.[1]

- The average American household carries over $15,000 in credit card debt.[2]

- The average U.S. household debt is 136 percent of household income, which means the typical American family owes far more money than it makes in an entire year.[3]

- The number of shopping centers in the U.S. surpassed the number of high schools back in 1987.[4]

- Women will spend more than eight years of their lives shopping.[5]

- The average size of the American home has more than doubled over the past 50 years.[6]

- One out of every 10 households in our country rents a storage unit to house its excess belongings.[7]

We live in a world that loves accumulating possessions. And while nobody would ever admit that they are trying to purchase happiness at their local department store, most people live like they are.

But what if there was a far better way to live life? One that recognizes the empty promises of advertisements and consumerism. One that champions the pursuit of living with only the most essential possessions needed for life. One that boldly declares there is more joy in owning less than can be found in pursuing more.

That truth would change everything about us. It would change the way we spend our hours, our energy, and our money. It would change where we focus our attention and our minds. It would change the very foundation of our lives.

In short, it would free us up to pursue the things in life of lasting value. It would be a completely life-changing and life-giving realization. And it may just line up with everything your heart, deep down, has been telling you all along.

PART 1:

JESUS' STORY

CHAPTER 1:

JESUS AND THE OFFER OF ABUNDANT LIFE

One Saturday afternoon, we took our young son to a large (and famous) toy store to spend some gift certificates he had received for his birthday. He wanted a skateboard. I liked the idea of having a boy that could hold his own on a skateboard, so we climbed in the car and made the drive to the local shopping center.

As soon as we walked into the store, my son noticed the almost limitless shelves of shiny, colorful toys. I saw his eyes get noticeably large as we began making our way through the store. He began considering all the possibilities. I had hoped to make a beeline for the sports section to pick out his skateboard, but I immediately realized that this shopping trip was not going to happen as I'd envisioned. He had become far too distracted by all of the possibilities.

Every single toy seemed to bring bigger and brighter smiles to each child playing with it—at least, that's what was depicted on the colorful packaging.

As we continued walking (I mean, as I was pulling him to keep him moving), my son quickly noticed an aisle with dinosaurs. Right on the end of the aisle, he spotted a pop-up tent that was designed to look like a cave. On the package was a young boy smiling from ear to ear while playing with 15-20 dinosaurs around the cave. At that very moment, my son decided that he no longer wanted a skateboard; he wanted a pop-up tent that looked like a dinosaur cave instead.

As his father, I had to step in. After all, I'm smart enough to realize that this pop-up tent was not a wise use of his limited birthday money. Anyone could easily see that this cheaply made tent would get played with once or twice and never again. It would likely break right away. But even if it didn't break right away, my son would have quickly realized it wasn't really that exciting (I mean, the dinosaurs weren't even included). Through some heavy persuasion techniques, I talked him out of the dinosaur cave and back to his original intent of a skateboard (that experience looks much better on paper than it did in the store; the actual events included much more kicking and screaming).

I'm glad I was there to play the father role and save my son from wasting his birthday money on that unwise purchase. I've been around longer and I've seen firsthand which toys get played with and which toys don't. I know enough about craftsmanship to better judge which toys will last and which will break. And I was able to make objective judgments about the situation. As a result, I knew that in the long run, he would find more enjoyment in a skateboard than a pretend dinosaur cave.

But this book isn't about him, it's about me— and it's about you.

The whole situation got me thinking. What about me? Who do I have in my life to keep me from making foolish decisions with my money and with my life? Oh sure, I do have more life experience and wisdom than my son, which gives me some discretion. But as I look around my house at all the things that seemed like a good purchase at the time (outdated clothes, dusty decorations, unused kitchen gadgets), I can't help but wonder if my house (and bank account) would look far different if I had somebody looking over my shoulder playing the father role, keeping me from wasteful spending.

But it's not just financial purchases that I regret; there are also life decisions that I regret. Actions that I regret. Words that never should have been said. Who in my life has the wisdom, love, and relationship to help me navigate the difficult waters of life?

TRAGIC MISCONCEPTIONS

There are many misconceptions about the person of Jesus floating around our world. I suppose this is to be expected. After all, a world that is set against Jesus is going to try everything it can to turn people away from him. And if the world can accomplish this by misrepresenting who Jesus is and what Jesus taught, it would make perfect sense that it would do just that.

One of the most tragic misrepresentations that the world will claim against Jesus is that his life only holds value for the afterlife. In other words, the culture will try to convince us that he holds great promise for the future, but little significance for today. If the world can convince us that Jesus was right about life in heaven, but wrong about life today, we will neglect most of his teaching that concerns our everyday life (morality, purpose, sacrifice, relationships). We may trust him for eternal life after death but believe his instructions for life today are wrong, outdated, boring, or downright impossible.

But Jesus told us otherwise. In John 10:10, Jesus made it very clear that he brought with him a new life for us today—a new and better way to enjoy our life right now. He said it like this: *"The thief comes only to steal and kill and destroy; I have come that they may have life, and have it to the full."*

Take a closer look at that statement. Jesus invites us to a new and better life today. His invitation was not just to enjoy God's best in eternity; it also was an invitation to enjoy God's best today. Jesus came so that we could enjoy the best possible life right now!

That is why the world's misconception about Christ is so damaging. If the world can convince you Jesus is not worth following today, it can keep you from living a life that experiences full happiness, hope, peace, love, and abundance. But more than that, this lie can keep you from making this world a better place and being an influence for God's kingdom during your life. If the world can convince you its way of life is better, it has won (at least for now).

But it would be foolish to trust God for unparalleled joy and bliss for all eternity, but not trust him for the best life today. If God created us, he knows what is best for our lives. And if God loves us, he would desire to lead us to the best possible life. If those two things are true of God, he becomes the best father figure ever, leading us wisely through the toy store of life to find the most lasting joy available.

GOD CREATED US

When I was in high school, I was required to take a speech class. At the time, I hated it. I can remember lying in bed the night before my speech scared to death, unable to sleep, and praying for snow. When the snow didn't come, I can remember sitting in class hoping that the person in front of me would accidentally give a 50-minute speech rather than a five-minute speech so time would run out and the bell would ring. Needless to say, that never happened. And speech class has forever been recorded on my permanent record as the lowest grade I ever received in high school.

But despite all the anxiety and terror that the class rained down on my life for those five months of my junior year, I still learned a lot about public speaking, confidence, and persuasive presentations. Early in the class, way before any of us gave our first presentation, we were given this piece of advice from the teacher: "Pick a topic that you are qualified to speak about. And early in your speech, tell your audience why you are qualified to speak about it." In fact, it was even the first item on our teacher's checklist for grading our speeches: "Did the speaker explain why he/she is qualified to give this speech?"

It became an important principle that I have never forgotten and have used throughout life in writing, conversations, and public speeches: "Pick a topic you are qualified to speak about. And be sure to explain to your audience why they should listen to you."

Perhaps, that is why God began the Bible the way he did. *In the beginning God created the heavens and the earth (Genesis 1:1).* In those 10 words, God establishes himself as perfectly (and solely) qualified to speak on all matters of life and death. God is the author and creator of life. By the simple sound of God's voice, the heavens and the earth and everything inside of them were created. Paul later tells us in the book of Colossians that everything was created by God and for God (Colossians 1:16).

God alone is the great creator of all things.

And this truth is entirely life-changing in every aspect. It means God alone is perfectly qualified to fix our lives, to direct our lives, and to enable us to make the most of them. After all, God made them in the first place!

Because God created life and knows best how it should be lived, it makes sense that the advice he gives concerning how it should be lived would carry extra weight in our decisions.

But there's more. Not only did God create life itself, he also loves us and wants us to experience the greatest possible good during it.

GOD LOVES US

One of the most repeated themes throughout Scripture is the truth that God loves us and desires to be intimately involved in each of our lives. God knows this truth is one that must be repeated until it is believed because the power behind this message is so life-transforming.

Assume for just a moment that you are about to get married. And you happen to find yourself in a most unique circumstance. You have the option of choosing between two people who you know want to marry you. To make the story even more interesting, let's say these two people are identical twins— identical in almost every imaginable way. They look exactly the same. They have exactly the same interests. Exactly the same intelligence, personality, talents, skills, hobbies, wardrobe, and so on, and so on. And by the way, for the sake of argument, they happen to be everything that you have ever wanted in a spouse: physically attractive, tidy, love to clean, love to cook, love to shovel the walk and mow the lawn (they even love to cheer against the New York Yankees). It doesn't matter—insert anything you want in the list to create your perfect spouse.

Of course, now we know the situation is hypothetical because I'm already taken—just kidding.

Your choice is between two virtually perfect people. There is really only one difference between them to help you decide: One loves you and one hates you. Twin A loves you with an incredible love. A love that you know is so abundant you can't even get your mind around it, much less your arms. This person's love for you is so great you cannot figure out why they would love you so much—but they do. They know everything about you—yet love you unconditionally with an extravagant love. They will do whatever it takes to bring you joy and to bring you peace. They'd even go so far as to lay down their own life for you.

Twin B, on the other hand, hates you. I mean, legitimately hates you. Hates you with the same passion and intensity that Twin A loves you. Twin B wants nothing more than to make your life miserable—to bring misery upon you and ultimately contribute to your death and destruction. And they are going to do everything in their power to make that happen. Oh, they don't come right out and tell you that (that would be too easy)—instead, they try to look similar on the outside by giving the same promises as Twin A. But you've been around long enough to see this, you've seen this twin's effect on others, and you've heard enough stories that you suspect it to be true.

So there you have it. Those are your choices. Which twin gets your wedding ring? Twin A or Twin B? This could be the easiest question you get asked all day.

You're going to choose to marry the one who loves you and wants the best for you—that would be the best way to live your life. It would be foolish to marry the one you know wants your destruction. Nice, fun story—I like telling it. But here's the reality. We really only have two options with our lives. We can choose to follow our selfish desires brought on by sin and the Evil One and encouraged by this world. Or we can choose God. We can choose to follow Christ. We can choose his will for our life and his plan for our actions.

And suddenly, our hypothetical situation becomes a little less hypothetical and a lot more real for every single one of us. Who gets your life's wedding ring? Wouldn't it make perfect sense to give your life over to the one who loved you enough to give his own life for you?

God loves you. God created you. God wants your best and knows what that is. God alone is worthy of our trust. And God has invited us to enjoy the abundant life in relationship with him *today*.

CHAPTER 2:
JESUS AND POSSESSIONS

Jesus loves me and wants what is best for me today (and throughout eternity). Yet his teachings on money and possessions seem to run contrary to what our culture says about how to experience the best today. I know his words proved to be very difficult for me while I was growing up.

Jesus holds a far different view on possessions than the world. I believe he holds a far different view on possessions than many churches. And I believe he holds a far different view on possessions than many Christians.

Over the course of this chapter, I want to examine four bold statements contained in the New Testament that directly relate to the accumulation of possessions. You may not agree with all of my conclusions about these verses, but I encourage you to consider what they reveal about Jesus' perspective on possessions.

LUKE 6:20

Looking at his disciples, he said: "Blessed are you who are poor, for yours is the kingdom of God."

When I was serving as a student ministry intern at a church in Nebraska, I was given a passage of Scripture to teach to a large room of high school students. It was summertime and the high school pastor was going to be away on vacation, so I was asked to fill in for him on this particular evening.

He had been teaching through the life of Jesus in the book of Luke, and I was assigned the next passage in Luke 6. In this specific chapter, Luke writes his account of Jesus' famous Sermon on the Mount.

I was completely blown away the very first time I read it. *Blessed are **the poor**?* Really? The statement didn't make any sense to me—what blessing is there to be found in poverty? This can't actually be true, I thought to myself. So I went on a personal journey to discover what Jesus really meant.

I began asking many of the well-respected, godly men and women in my life the following question: "What did Jesus mean when he said, 'Blessed are the poor?' " Most of them answered the same way.

First, they would tell me that Jesus wasn't talking about financial poverty; he was referring to spiritual poverty. After all, he couldn't possibly have meant it would be a blessing to be financially poor. To prove their point, they would direct me to Matthew 5:3, where Matthew offers his account of the Sermon on the Mount. Matthew phrases it this way: *"Blessed are the poor in spirit, for theirs is the kingdom of heaven."* "You see," they would say, "Jesus was clearly teaching us about spiritual poverty, not financial poverty."

Yet despite all my conversations, I could never get past the fact that Luke didn't write,

"Blessed are the poor in spirit." He wrote, "Blessed are the poor." And he must have had a reason.

LUKE 18:18-23

A certain ruler asked him, "Good teacher, what must I do to inherit eternal life?"

"Why do you call me good?" Jesus answered. "No one is good—except God alone. You know the commandments: 'You shall not commit adultery, you shall not murder, you shall not steal, you shall not give false testimony, honor your father and mother.'"

"All these I have kept since I was a boy," he said.

When Jesus heard this, he said to him, "You still lack one thing. Sell everything you have and give to the poor, and you will have treasure in heaven. Then come, follow me."

When he heard this, he became very sad, because he was very wealthy.

In Luke 18:18-23, we read the story of a rich young ruler who approached Jesus with one specific question: "How can I gain eternal life?"

After being told to keep the commandments, the young man responds, "Done. In fact, I've kept all of those ever since I was a young boy." When Jesus hears this, he says to him, "You're still missing something. Sell all your stuff and give that money to the poor, and you will have treasure in heaven. Then, come and follow me."

Over the years, I have heard this story taught countless times by various pastors in various places for various purposes. Preachers praise the rich young ruler for seeking out eternal life, they debate the reasoning for Jesus' response, they criticize the young man for his pride, or they speak on the implications of rejecting the offer of Christ.

But no matter what the main point of the sermon, nearly every pastor who preaches through this story holds one thing in common.

They are quick to point out that Jesus didn't really mean we must sell our possessions to follow him.

Instead, they tell me that Jesus was pointing out the one thing that was keeping this young man from following him. In this specific circumstance, the man's love for money and possessions was greater than his love for Jesus. The young man proved it by walking away, and Jesus made that statement simply as a means to specifically point out his weakness.

And while there may be truth in this application, is it possible that we who live privileged lives today have too easily dismissed Jesus' specific charge to "sell your possessions and give to the poor"?

MATTHEW 6:19-21

"Do not store up for yourselves treasures on earth, where moths and vermin destroy, and where thieves break in and steal. But store up for yourselves treasures in heaven, where moths and vermin do not destroy, and where

thieves do not break in and steal. For where your treasure is, there your heart will be also."

In Matthew 6:19-21, Jesus continues to teach us how to properly understand money and possessions in our life. He encourages us to not hoard treasures here on earth, but to stockpile them in heaven.

Again, this is a common verse taught in many churches and on countless Sunday mornings. Yet nearly every time I've heard it taught, the focus is directed toward *giving* and the *importance of laying up treasures in heaven*. Personally, I don't ever recall hearing a pastor charge an audience to specifically remove our "stockpiles" here on earth.

We are called to give financially to the church and we are called to lay up treasures in heaven, true. But in the exact same breath, Jesus warns us not to hoard treasures here on earth—unless two-story homes filled with overflowing closets and garages don't count as stockpiles. Personally, I'm not sure what else we'd call them.

LUKE 3:11

John answered, "Anyone who has two shirts should share with the one who has none, and anyone who has food should do the same."

In Luke 3, John the Baptist is preparing the way for the ministry of Christ by calling the people of Israel to repent and turn their hearts toward God once again. While he does, the crowd asks him, "What are we supposed to do?" John replies directly, "If you have two coats, give one away." And then he adds, "Do the same with your food."

If I read John's words plainly, one of the most important steps I can take to prepare my heart for God's work is to remove the extra possessions that are keeping me from him. As followers of Christ, we ought to be taking whatever steps we possibly can to prepare our hearts for God's kingdom to take root.

This verse isn't taught frequently, and when it is taught, it often is an encouragement to be generous in our abundance instead of a verse to be applied in full truth. After all, in a country where the number of television sets in the average home outnumbers the people living in it,[8] this can be an incredibly inconvenient teaching.

How then can Jesus' plain teachings on money and possessions be consistent with his invitation to a full and abundant life? Are these statements given as a test of my faith? Are they a call to sacrifice the things of this world for joy in the afterlife? Or could they really be instructions for a better way to live?

To help you understand how I answer those questions, there is another story I need to tell you. Mine.

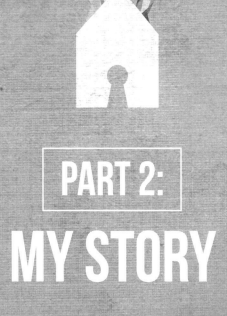

PART 2:

MY STORY

CHAPTER 3:

A PRETTY TYPICAL STORY OF TOO MUCH STUFF

It was a beautiful three-day weekend at our home in suburban Vermont. The sun was shining, the flowers were blooming, the grass was beginning to green, and the trees were budding.

My wife and I woke up early that Saturday with one goal in mind: spring-clean the entire house. We had decided to spend a large chunk of our three-day holiday weekend cleaning the house from top to bottom. After all, that's what families do, right? My specific responsibility would include the garage, which had been collecting snow and mud all winter long. I knew it was going to be an all-day project so I set my alarm early to get a good start.

We are, by definition, just your standard, run-of-the-mill, middle-class family of four living in the suburbs. My wife and I are in our 30s. My son is 9, my daughter, 6. I have served as a youth pastor in two different churches over the past 14 years. We are almost everything typical (minus the dog and the white picket fence).

It all started routinely enough that Saturday morning as my son and I began to clean out that garage. I had asked my son, Salem, to help me. At the time, he was only 5 years old, but I thought he could certainly help pull out some of his toys into the driveway to make the cleaning and organizing easier. I was surprised to find him so eager to help—that was, until he found his baseball and glove lying in the very first box of toys. Within two minutes of beginning my project, my boy was in the backyard begging me to come play catch with him.

But I had a job to do. I promised him I would play after the garage was clean, and I meant it. I just didn't realize how long it would take me to finish.

Nearly four hours later, I was still working on the same garage. My son was still in the backyard asking me to play. My neighbors also happened to be outside at the same time, planting gardens, watering flowers, and tending to the outside of their two-level home. My neighbor, noticing my frustration with the project, turned to me and said sarcastically, "Ahh, the joys of home ownership."

Sensing her sarcasm, I responded, "Well, you know what they say, 'The more stuff you own, the more your stuff owns you.' " Her next sentence struck a chord with my mind, heart, and soul, and changed the course of my life forever.

She responded, "That's why my daughter is a minimalist. She keeps telling me I don't need to own all this stuff!"

Up until that point in my life, I had never heard the term *minimalist* before. Yet somehow, it was the one word that defined a desire that had been building in my heart. It was, after all, incredibly obvious that my possessions were keeping me from doing what I most wanted to be doing that day: playing with my boy. I quickly ran inside to tell my wife about my short conversation. Her response was the same as mine: "Minimalism, huh? We don't have to own all this stuff? I sure think that would solve a lot of our problems."

I immediately went to the computer (garage still unfinished) and began researching the idea of minimalism. I found a variety of websites describing a simple lifestyle focused on owning just the essentials of life and removing the clutter. Examples of people living a minimalist life could be found all over the world: a couple in Portland, a father with six kids living in San Francisco, a young man traveling the world. The more I read, the more I noticed one consistent theme in their stories: freedom. The more I considered the practical benefits of intentionally owning fewer possessions, the more I desired their lifestyle. In that moment, a minimalist was born.

WHY MINIMALISM WAS AN EASY CHOICE FOR US

Now, almost four years later, I can look back and see why minimalism was an easy choice for me and why it resonated with my soul from the very beginning.

- **There are a number of things in life I value more than possessions.** I value God. I value my family. I value my opportunity as a pastor to shape students' lives. I value my friendships. I value character, morality, and spiritual maturity. I desire each of those far more than worldly possessions. And seeking them is a far better use of my energy.

- **I enjoy clean, tidy, uncluttered rooms—but don't like to clean.** I want things to be clean but hate putting in the effort to make it a reality. I can only assume I'm not the only one. Minimalism scratches that itch. Owning fewer possessions helps keep messes to a minimum. And the messes that do arise are easy to clean up.

- **I enjoy minimalist design in most things.** From clothes and watches to art and interior design, if it is modern and sleek, I generally love it. Minimalist design is not a prerequisite for owning fewer possessions, but in my case, it made the transition easier.

- **We love to entertain.** My job as a pastor keeps our house bubbling with excitement. At one point in our ministry, we had three different groups routinely meeting in our living room. Living with less has allowed us to keep our house presentable at all times.

- **I don't fear change.** Living with less was definitely a life-changing choice for us. It was a countercultural lifestyle that was going to require us to live differently from those around us. Fortunately, early in my life, I made a conscious decision that I didn't need to live my life like everyone else lived theirs.

- **I realize money can hold great value.** Our money is only as valuable as how we choose to spend it. If I spend my money on cookies or chips, it's worth a tasty little snack. If I choose to spend my money on a fancy home, it's worth nothing more than a big building made of brick or lumber. But if I spend my money on investments of eternal worth (such as relationships, justice, or others), it becomes far more valuable than cookies, cars, or fancy houses. It begins to take on eternal value, and its worth will far outlive me.

You may identify with one or two of the reasons I just listed. If so, you can probably agree with me that living with fewer possessions may be an easy choice. If you do not directly identify with any of our reasons and still have some doubts, just keep reading. A simple, minimal lifestyle has benefits for all.

Since becoming minimalists, we have sold, donated, or discarded almost 70 percent of our worldly possessions. We moved to a smaller house. But more importantly, we have saved money, reduced clutter, and removed distractions. Our home is cleaner.

Our three-day weekends are spent together as a family, not cleaning the garage. And we are living far happier lives because of it.

Our only regret is not finding this way of living earlier.

CHAPTER 4:

AN INTRODUCTION TO A NEW WAY OF LIFE

Many people I speak with get nervous when they hear the term *minimalist*. For them, it conjures up images of no iPads®, no cool clothes, no sports, and no fun. Rightly so, they decide that is no way to enjoy life. Believe me, I agree—that is no way to enjoy life.

We live in the suburbs of a large city. We have two small children. We are active in our community. We love to entertain and show hospitality. I love to play basketball, tennis, and golf. While not exceptional, our life is not identical to anybody else. It is our life—nobody else's. And if we were going to become minimalists, it would have to be a style of minimalism specific to us. It would require us to ask questions, to practice some give-and-take, to identify what we most value, and to be humble enough to change course when necessary.

Eventually, we defined minimalism for our life in four aspects:

- **WE WILL INTENTIONALLY PROMOTE THE THINGS WE MOST VALUE.** The heart of our minimalism can be summed up in this phrase: *It is the intentional promotion of the things we most value and the removal of anything that distracts us from it.* This promotion can be seen in how we spend our time, the artwork that we display, and even the clothes that we wear. But most importantly, it involves removing the unnecessary physical possessions from our lives that are preventing us from fulfilling our greatest purposes.

- **WE WILL REMOVE ALL "CLUTTER" FROM OUR LIVES.** This process began with physical items as we moved from room to room selling, donating, and recycling everything that we no longer used. As we did, we realized that simplicity and order bring freedom, happiness, and balance. Our home began to give life rather than drain it (perhaps some of you with cluttered bedrooms can relate). As we began clearing physical clutter from our lives, we noticed opportunities to remove other nonphysical clutter from our lives: time commitments that weren't beneficial, emotional clutter that was defining our present, even some spiritual clutter (incorrect views of God) that was tainting our view of him. Since then, it has become far easier to recognize the clutter and remain free from it in all aspects of life.

- **WE WILL USE OUR MONEY FOR THINGS MORE VALUABLE THAN PHYSICAL POSSESSIONS.** Advertisers have controlled our finances for too long. Since the day we were born, they have told us what needs to be bought, when it needs to be purchased, and what store we should visit to find the best value. When our family chose to live differently, we broke the control that our consumer-driven society had over us. Suddenly, we became free to use our finances to pursue endeavors far greater than those offered at our local department store. We have used our money to support orphanages around the world, to help launch new Christian artists, to furnish coffee shops in Mongolia, and to assist local charities. And each of these endeavors has provided us with a far greater sense of happiness than buying more things to put in our closet.

- **WE WILL LIVE A COUNTERCULTURAL LIFE THAT IS ATTRACTIVE TO OTHERS.** We have met many minimalists over the past two years that live a life far from attractive to us. They have sold all their possessions to live communally on a farm. No thanks. They have listed all their possessions on a sheet of paper and determined to eliminate all but 100. No thanks. They have gotten rid of all their furniture to sit on the floor in an empty room. Definitely no thanks. Instead, we have determined to live out a rational minimalism with fewer possessions that fits our lifestyle, reflects our values, and invites others to simplify their lives as well. Minimalism is not a decision to live with nothing. It is a decision to live with only the essential.

This is an essential idea: Our particular practice of living with less is going to look different from everyone else's. It must! After all, we live a completely different life than anyone else.

Similarly, if you decide to intentionally live with less, it is going to look completely different from someone else who chooses to live with less. You may grow up to have a large family, small family, or no family. You may end up living on a farm, in a house, or in a studio apartment. You may love music, movies, or books. You may cherish old photographs, family heirlooms, or romantic letters from a lover. You may work as a banker, a mechanic, an artist, or a missionary. Your life is going to look completely unique.

Find a style of minimalism—or whatever word you're most comfortable with when explaining the idea of living with less—that works for you. One that is not cumbersome, but freeing based on your values, desires, passions, and rational thinking. Be aware that your definition will not come overnight. It will take time. It will evolve, even change with you as your life changes. It will require give-and-take. You will make a few mistakes along the way. And so, it will also require humility.

You certainly don't have it all figured out today. That's totally OK. The most important thing right now is to intentionally realize the burden that excessive possessions can place on our lives and commit to living an intentional life with only the most essential.

PART 3

YOUR STORY

CHAPTER 5:
OUR ACTIONS FOLLOW OUR HEART

Goals move us, and goals shape us. Our goals change us and affect the way we go live our lives.

My friend Katherine had a goal in mind. I knew her in high school when her desire was to earn a diving scholarship from the local big-name university. All through her high school years, this goal motivated her in incredible ways. It inspired her to wake up early in the morning and hit the gym. It inspired her every day after school as she was in the pool diving over and over again, for hours at a time. It affected her eating habits, causing her to choose healthy salads and bottled water rather than fast food and soda (like I was eating and drinking). She would go to bed rehearsing dives in her mind, and she would wake up thinking about them and what she needed to work on that day. Her goal of making the college diving team affected nearly every aspect of her life.

That was, until the spring of her senior year, when she was notified that despite all her hard work, she would not be receiving the diving scholarship she desperately desired. She had poured her heart and soul into realizing that goal, but it had vanished and was out of her reach.

Overnight, Katherine became a different person. Once she realized this goal was not meant to be, her life changed drastically and radically. Suddenly, she began spending tons of time with her friends, hanging out after school, and staying later at our parties. She started ordering cheeseburgers and soda instead of salads and water (which made us feel better about ourselves, too). She began sleeping in on weekends instead of hitting the gym at 6 a.m. It was almost as if she had a different life before and after the death of her goal. She became a completely different person.

Katherine's story reminds me of one of life's simple truths. Our actions will always follow the true desire of our heart. What our heart believes and loves always determines the path of our life. Our deeply held goals always shape the life we end up living. This truth applies to all areas of life: our energy, our time, our relationships, our spirituality, our money, and our possessions.

Before any of us would choose to intentionally live with fewer possessions—especially in a world that always desires more—we must be convinced that the lifestyle is worth our effort.

HOW SIMPLICITY APPEALS TO THE HEART

Jim Carrey, the incredibly popular actor, once said, "I think everybody should get rich and famous and do everything they ever dreamed of so they can see that it's not the answer."[9] Though I have never become rich or famous, I can still relate to the point he was trying to make. Gaining all the possessions in the world won't make us happy. We were created for something greater.

Over the past several years since deciding to live with fewer possessions, I have had the privilege to write and speak often on the topic. The simple message that there is "more joy in pursuing less than can be found in pursuing more" has been presented to audiences in various venues, has been discussed in small group settings throughout the country, and remains a constant conversation piece in my personal relationships wherever I go.

And through it all, almost surprisingly, I have found the message of simplicity to be universally appealing. In fact, the number of people who have told me that I am wrong and have flat-out argued against me can be counted on my fingers (that's less than 10), and I distinctly remember each of them.

I have come to believe and understand that minimalism—the intentional promotion of the things I most value and the removal of everything that distracts me from it—is a message that appeals to the heart and resonates with the soul because God never created us to hoard possessions. As a result, the invitation to live with fewer possessions is appreciated, desired, and often accepted when offered.

Living with less appeals to our hearts because...

- **The heart knows that possessions don't equal joy.** We know intuitively that happiness is not found in owning more. Instead, happiness is found in the pursuit of the lasting passions that God has placed in our hearts.

- **The heart recognizes freedom when we experience it.** Possessions burden us, often far more than we realize. The heart desperately longs for freedom and the opportunity to be associated with things of true value.

- **The heart knows its resources are limited.** Money, time, energy, and focus are finite resources. We do not contain an infinite amount of any. Therefore, we must make intentional decisions about where they are allocated. And our heart has little desire to spend them all on something as empty and fleeting as owning more things.

- **The heart knows truth.** Most people in our world are living a lie. They are passionately pursuing things of finite nature. Society, culture, and advertisements promise lasting fulfillment in bigger houses, nicer cars, and trendier clothes. But lasting fulfillment can never be found in temporal pursuits. It can only be found in God.

- **The heart knows when it is being fake.** Oftentimes, we collect possessions just to put on an outward façade to those around us that our life is successful, put together, and all figured out. But deep down, we know it is not. And in the deepest places of our hearts, we desire to stop pretending and to start being completely real and vulnerable—for the first time in a long time.

- **The heart finds joy in lasting value.** *So we fix our eyes not on what is seen, but on what is unseen, since what is seen is temporary, but what is unseen is eternal (2 Corinthians 4:18).* Our souls desire to live for the things that matter by finding joy in the invisible things that cannot be purchased with money.

- **The heart longs for the higher attributes.** We desire contentment, generosity, gratitude, and self-control. We were created to live life displaying these fruits. We want our lives to be described and remembered by those words—not merely by the things we owned. And the intentional reduction of possessions allows greater opportunity for these positive heart habits to emerge.

Unfortunately, we have been deceived. As a society, we have too easily believed the lie that there is more happiness in owning more. But we all know it's not true—our heart has been arguing for less all along.

It's time we stop chasing empty pursuits and start listening to the heart that knows us best.

This book is written to introduce you to what I have found as a key to happiness: living with less. But for this pursuit to become a reality in anybody's life (yours or mine), we must be convinced that this lifestyle is worth our effort. And in a consumer-driven world where we see 5,000 advertisements every day,[10] if our heart is not fully convinced, we will struggle with the same old pattern of life that defines so many of the people around us.

We must be persuaded that there are benefits in living with less. For that reason, the entire next chapter is dedicated solely to clearly defining how living with fewer possessions can bring greater joy, comfort, and freedom into your life. It is written to turn your heart from the empty pursuit of physical possessions.

CHAPTER 6:

THE LIFE-CHANGING BENEFITS OF OWNING LESS

As we began removing the unnecessary possessions from our home and lives, we began to see the practical benefits that it brought. We quickly noticed that these benefits were not unique to us. In fact, they are available to anyone who will reject the world's system of accumulating more.

Some benefits were particularly meaningful to us. We found great financial relief in owning less. We suddenly had far more time available to spend with our family. We had extra energy to direct toward our students and the things we most valued. And we found far more opportunity to pursue our greatest passions.

BENEFIT #1: SAVE MONEY / REDUCE DEBT

One benefit of living simply is the very practical reality that it costs less. As you accumulate fewer things, you spend less money. There are far too many people in the world who believe the secret to financial freedom is earning more money. Unfortunately, when they begin to make more money without spending restraints in place, they often just spend more money as their income grows. As a result, people all around us are held captive to debt. So much so, an entire industry has arisen promising to help people get out of debt (you've seen the commercials). In reality, the reverse is truer: The real secret to financial freedom is spending less. Buying less stuff is a practical solution to (almost) every money problem. If you live a life committed to accumulating less stuff, you will spend less.

BENEFIT #2: LIVE IN A SMALL SPACE

According to statistics, the average house size in America has doubled since the 1950s[11]— yet how many times have you heard someone complain their house is still too small? Chances are pretty good that our houses aren't too small—perhaps we've just put too much stuff inside them.

For most families, a house is the costliest investment they'll ever make—almost 40 percent of an average American's expenses go toward housing costs.[12] Being able to live comfortably in a smaller home can provide far more financial flexibility and stability.

BENEFIT #3: EASIER TO CLEAN

When we began to declutter the decorations in our living room, I was surprised at the amount of dust that I found on the shelves (particularly the top shelves). Clearly, the vast number of knickknacks on the shelving made the proposition of dusting a daunting task. When we finished decluttering our bedroom, we suddenly noticed that it took much less time to clean. When we began decluttering our wardrobe, we found it much easier to keep our closets tidy. A simple pattern began emerging: Own less stuff = Spend less time cleaning. This benefit holds true whether you are cleaning a bedroom, a closet, a basement, or an entire house.

BENEFIT #4: EASIER TO FIND STUFF

I used to judge track and field at a local high school in Vermont. One particular morning before beginning our journey of living with less, I woke up to a steady rain on the day of the state's largest competition. And because track and field doesn't stop for rain, I knew it would be a good idea to bring my umbrella. That was until I started rummaging through the mess in our basement closet trying to find it.

If you've ever felt the panic that arises when you can't find something you desperately need and the time is slowly ticking away, you can relate to how I felt. Our closet was a big hodgepodge of winter clothes (snow boots, gloves, scarves, snow pants), spring clothes (rain boots, raincoats), outdoor toys, and board games all piled up in one small closet. At the end of the search, all I could find was a blue umbrella with the big logo of a woman on it. I ended up judging the largest track and field meet of the year with a girl's umbrella. Thankfully, this will never happen again. Own less clutter = Find things more quickly.

BENEFIT #5: LESS STRESS

The stress level in our country has reached epidemic proportions even though new technology to make our lives easier has grown rapidly. All these possessions we have invented, collected, and hoarded over the years to make our lives easier have not fulfilled their promise. Instead, we are worse off than we've ever been! Why?

It's because clutter (our excessive possessions) is a form of visual distraction, and everything in our vision pulls at our attention at least a little. The less clutter, the less visual stress we have in our environments. A simple home is calming.

I have found this to be true and you will, too, with a simple experiment. In your mind, compare two rooms in your home—one that is clear of clutter (maybe a formal living room, guest bedroom, or tidy linen closet) and one that is cluttered (maybe the basement, attic, garage, or your room). Consider each of them separately. What is your internal emotional response to each of the rooms? Doesn't the clear one bring about a calming effect while the cluttered room arouses emotions of distraction or anxiety? Which emotion would you prefer to define your life? It's absolutely true: Own less stuff = Experience less stress.

BENEFIT #6: GOOD FOR THE ENVIRONMENT

Assume for a moment that you have a mom who does all the work around the house for you. Every morning after you wake up, she makes your bed. Your laundry is always clean and folded. Your kitchen is spotless. She even cleans and vacuums your room for you when you are gone at school. You make the mess, she cleans it up. Always.

If that were the case, how would you show the most respect and honor to your mother? Would you best bring her honor by trying on all your clothes and making as large a mess as possible for her to clean? Or would you bring her honor by organizing all your things, putting dirty clothes away, and keeping the room as close to clean as possible?

The second one, of course. You would bring honor to her by sustaining the perfection that she desires for you as much as possible. That's how I look at the environment. If God created it in a state of perfection (the Garden of Eden) and will renew it again to a state of perfection (Romans 8:19-21), we would best bring honor to God and God's creation by taking special care of the earth today. The less we consume, the less damage we do to the environment. And that benefits everyone.

BENEFIT #7: MORE TIME FOR THE THINGS THAT MATTER MOST

John Ruskin, an art critic in the 19th century, once wrote, "Every increased possession loads us with a new weariness."[13] He was right. Every single thing you own requires a little bit of your attention and time whether it be researching, shopping, cleaning, organizing, repairing, replacing, recycling, or working just to make the money to buy the new thing that you can take home to clean and organize and replace. John Ruskin was right. The more stuff you own, the more your stuff owns you.

That's why those who live a simpler lifestyle have more time on their hands for other things in life. It was this benefit that ultimately led to our decision to become minimalists. Remember the story of my son playing baseball in the backyard while I was stuck cleaning the garage?

We have found that living with fewer possessions means that all our belongings have a standard place where they belong in our home, which makes cleaning a snap. I spend less time searching for books, keys, and shoes. In short, I spend far less time being the janitor for my possessions, and far more time doing the things I love.

BENEFIT #8: BE HAPPIER

Owning fewer possessions makes you happier. According to a survey by the Simplicity Institute, an organization that surveyed 2,500 people across various countries who self-identified themselves as living with fewer possessions, 87 percent of respondents indicated they were happier now than when they owned more possessions.[14] This may sound contrary to everything we've been told growing up. But when we begin to consider the benefits of living with less (less debt, less stress, less cleaning), it begins to make sense why these statistics would hold true. Happiness is not found in owning as many possessions as possible; it's found in living a life consistent with your greatest passions.

BENEFIT #9: PICK A CAREER YOU LOVE

Confucius, an ancient Chinese philosopher, is credited with saying, "Choose a job you love, and you will never have to work a day in your life." One of the reasons I was so excited to write a book for students is because teenagers have their entire lives ahead of them. You are making choices today that will chart the course for the rest of your life—as opposed to most adults, whose lives have already been determined by the choices they made when they were younger. A teenager who embraces the idea of living with less opens his or her life to endless possibilities—including picking a passion as a career.

Somebody who decides to intentionally live with less has less need to hold a certain level of income. As a result, they can choose whatever career path they most desire. Their decision does not have to be dictated by income level. And while there is nothing unbiblical about earning money, when your salary package can be removed from the career-choice equation, you are free to choose your career based on other factors—such as "something I really want to do."

I have tons of friends in their mid-30s still paying off tens of thousands of dollars in student loans. Many of them are stuck in jobs they no longer enjoy just so they can earn enough money to pay off the debt associated with learning their career in the first place. And while some of these circumstances cannot be entirely avoided, making wise choices about your career (and college) today will save you decades of burden in the future. Own less stuff = Choose a career you love.

BENEFIT #10: FREEDOM FROM THE COMPARISON GAME

Our culture begs us to own more. Advertisements call us to purchase the latest and the greatest. Our natural tendencies cause us to compare our lives with those around us. Add in the fact that we seem to have a built-in desire to impress others by owning as much as possible. And you've got a recipe for disaster.

As a result, we spend precious energy comparing our stuff to others. We notice what she got for her birthday, what technology he carries in his pocket, or what trendy clothes all of our friends seem to be wearing. Ultimately, we end up wishing we had more. But this constant dreaming, hoping, and envying others' possessions steal from our joy and contentment today. We spend so much mental energy thinking about what we *don't* own, we fail to appreciate the things that we *do* own. It makes us feel we are missing out on something—even though there is so much joy right in front of us.

BENEFIT #11: LESS LIKELY TO BE INFLUENCED BY A CONSUMERISTIC CULTURE

My family of four still owns three beds, three dressers, two couches, one table with chairs, eight plates, eight bowls, eight glasses. We may be seeking to live a minimalist life, but we are still consumers. After all, to live is to consume.

But we have worked hard to escape excessive consumerism. For us, shopping becomes excessive when it extends beyond what is needed. Why? When people begin consuming more than they need, boundaries are removed. Personal credit allows people to make purchases beyond their income level. Advertisements subtly reshape desires around material possessions. And the consumption culture that surrounds all of us begins to make excessive consumption appear natural and normal.

Excessive consumption leads to bigger houses, faster cars, trendier clothes, fancier technology, and overfilled drawers. It promises happiness but never delivers. Instead, it results in a desire for more—a desire that is promoted by the world around us. And it slowly begins robbing us of life. It redirects our God-given passions to things that can never fulfill. It consumes our limited resources. And it is time that we escape the vicious cycle.

BENEFIT #12: FEWER PLACES FOR YOUR HEART TO GO

In Matthew 6:21, Jesus says, *"For where your treasure is, there your heart will be also."* The heart will always follow our greatest investments—whether it's our car, our house, our career, or our wardrobe. We tie our hearts to certain things by the sheer amount of investment we put into them. And too many of us are tying our hearts to the wrong things. We are devoting our lives and tying our hearts to material possessions that will never last. Lasting fulfillment can never be tied to things that are temporal by nature.

Instead, we ought to invest our money, time, and lives in things that are truly important. Invest in knowing God, your family, your friends, or the causes that you believe in. And as you do, you'll notice that your heart naturally begins to be drawn to them more and more.

The spell of materialism can be hard to break. As long as we live on earth surrounded by material possessions, keeping them in proper perspective is going to be a struggle. But we can begin to break the fascination with things by reminding ourselves that we are investing more than our dollars into them. We are tying our very hearts to them as well.

BENEFIT #13: AN EXAMPLE TO OTHERS

The Bible holds great promise for us regardless of our age. In fact, in 1 Timothy 4:12, Paul gives a special instruction of inspiration to his young reader. He says this: *Don't let anyone look down on you because you are young, but set an example for the believers in speech, in conduct, in love, in faith and in purity.* Paul knew our lives could influence others regardless of age. When we begin to live simpler lives and reject the common pattern of trying to accumulate as much as possible, we become powerful examples to those around us. Our choices (and reasoning behind them) will begin to change the lives of our friends, our family, and our churches.

PURSUE YOUR PASSION

We were created to live our lives in pursuit of our greatest passions. Whatever those passions may be (art, music, travel, entrepreneurship, friends, relationships, family, missions), very few of us would ever say that "owning stuff" is our greatest desire. Instead, we desire to discover love, find meaning, and live our lives for something bigger than ourselves. We desire to make an eternal difference in our world. Living with less provides that opportunity!

Consider again the list of benefits: more money, more time, more freedom, less stress, more happiness, less influence from the world around us. In other words, more opportunity to pursue your greatest passions in life— whatever they are!

And if that's not reason enough to intentionally live with fewer possessions, I don't know what is.

Our only regret is not finding this way of living earlier.

CHAPTER 7:

THE HEART IMPACT OF CHOOSING LESS

Four years ago, we decided to begin living with fewer possessions. At the time, our decision was based entirely on outward emotions. I was tired of the never-ending cleaning and organizing that my possessions required. I was tired of living paycheck to paycheck. And I was getting frustrated that I couldn't find enough time and energy to be with my family and the people that mattered most. Somehow, I had been unable to notice that my desire to own possessions was the cause of this discontent in my life. Luckily, my neighbor pointed it out with a simple statement: "Maybe you don't need to own all this stuff."

My life forever changed. Ultimately, it brought great resolution to the emotions listed above.

But it also provided me with even greater opportunity to change than I had ever imagined. The outward change of behavior has brought along with it the opportunity for inward change as well. It has allowed my very heart to change and adopt values I have always admired in others. Heart attitudes that were very evident in the life of Jesus have become more evident in my life.

For example, consider how the intentional decision to live with fewer possessions allows our hearts to embrace some of the most desirable qualities of life.

Contentment: *being mentally or emotionally satisfied with things as they are*

So much of the discontent in our lives revolves around physical possessions and comparing our things to what other people have. An intentional decision to live with less allows that discontent to slowly fade away. I become freed up to find happiness in my present circumstance.

Generosity: *willingness in giving away one's money, time, other resources*

When the selfish, hoarder-based mentality is removed from our thinking, we are free to use our resources for other purposes. We are allowed (and have more opportunity) to redirect our energy, time, and money elsewhere, supporting many of the causes (or people) we feel strongly about.

Gratitude: *a feeling of thankfulness or appreciation*

One of the most important steps that we can take toward experiencing gratitude is to think less about the things we don't have and spend more time focusing on the things we already do have. Intentionally living with less provides that opportunity by giving up the pursuit for more.

Self-Control: *the ability to exercise restraint or control over one's feelings, emotions, reactions*

Many people go through life having no clear sense of their true values. Instead, their desires are molded by the culture and the advertisements that bombard them each day. As a result, they find no consistency in life, no self-control. The decision to live your life apart from an ever-shifting culture provides the opportunity for self-control to emerge.

Honesty: *honorable in principles, intentions, and actions; upright and fair*

Many—not all, but many—of the lies and mistruths that are told in our society are based on a desire to get ahead and possess more. Finding contentment with your lot in life eliminates the need to be dishonest for financial gain.

Encouragement: *to inspire with hope, courage, or confidence*

As our desires stop focusing on others and what they have that we don't, we are more able to appreciate their accomplishments, their success, and the beauty that they bring to the world. We can fully appreciate others without being jealous of them (or worse, hoping for their downfall) and are more apt to encourage them to success.

Now, please don't misread me. I am not contending that minimalists are necessarily more content, generous, grateful, or honest than others. I know many incredibly generous people who would not describe themselves as minimalists. I'm sure there are some self-defined minimalists who would chart obnoxiously high on the selfishness meter. And I would never claim to have arrived fully in any of the categories listed above.

But I do believe with all my heart that intentionally living with less does allow greater opportunity for these positive heart habits to emerge. What you do with that opportunity is up to you.

CHAPTER 8:
A WORD TO THE SKEPTICS

Minimalists come in all sizes, ages, genders, races, nationalities, social classes, and religions. It is a growing movement that continues to invite others to live with less and define their lives in greater ways than by the things they own. It can be a path to experience a more Christ-like understanding of possessions. Yet despite its recent growth, it continues to be misunderstood by a percentage of the population.

With that in mind, I think it would be wise to personally address some of the common misconceptions about minimalism in case you are thinking any of them.

MINIMALISTS ARE BORING
A minimalist life is not void of excitement or entertainment. In fact, minimalism can reduce many of the mundane tasks

(organizing, shopping, cleaning) that rob us of daily excitement. And when unnecessary possessions have been removed, minimalists can be free to choose for themselves what things will define their lives. Some will choose to travel the world, find a new hobby, appreciate nature, get involved in their community, or spend more time with friends.

MINIMALISTS DON'T OWN NICE THINGS

Actually, one of the greatest unforeseen benefits not listed earlier is the opportunity to purchase possessions of higher quality. For some reason, many people don't correlate owning fewer things with owning nicer things. But the truth is, they go hand in hand and are directly related. When a commitment is made to buy fewer things, our lives are opened to the opportunity of owning nicer things as well. In fact, one of the key thoughts behind minimalism is that it is far better to own a few, quality things than a whole bunch of junk. This relates to technology, clothing, furniture, sporting equipment, and other areas.

MINIMALISTS ARE NOT SENTIMENTAL

Less is different from none. Personally, my family finds more value in sentimental belongings if we pull out the most important pieces and keep them in a significant place. As a result, rather than a box full of sentimental things stuck in the basement or attic, we display the most important sentimental pieces from our past somewhere in our home—again, promoting the things that are most valuable to us. Minimalism doesn't mean we had to throw away all of our sentimental belongings.

MINIMALISM IS TOO HARD

In a world that seeks to own more and accomplishes that by encouraging others to do the same, minimalism is countercultural. It is a lifestyle that goes against the mainstream belief about what constitutes happiness. In that way, it is difficult. It requires trust, intentionality, discipline, and frequent readjustments. It forces us to define our values and choose what is most important in life.

But it is not so hard that it can't be done. In fact, if my typical family of four can do it, so can you. There's nothing special about us. The only difference between you and me is that somebody took the time to introduce my family to a new way to live life. We reduced our possessions, discovered the joy that can only be found by living with less, and have never looked back.

No wonder minimalists come in all sizes, ages, genders, races, nationalities, social classes, and religions. And no wonder it is a growing movement that invites people to own less and define their lives in greater ways than by the things they own. They find freedom because of it.

PART 4:

THE INTERSECTION OF YOUR STORY AND JESUS' STORY

CHAPTER 9:

MAYBE JESUS HAS BEEN RIGHT ALL ALONG

A number of years ago I was watching a popular sports news channel on television when a story caught my eye. The reporter was recounting the story of a young football sensation named Larry. As the story unfolded, I learned that Larry came from a family of six in the Upper Midwest. The story was pretty typical except that Larry wasn't quite like the other kids in his high school. You see, two times a week after school and every Sunday he went to his job—as a ball boy for the Minnesota Vikings.

The Minnesota Vikings coach at the time, Dennis Green, had given Larry an opportunity to get off the streets and come to work for the Minnesota Vikings. All throughout high school, Larry had hung out with the players and the coaches and had developed great relationships with each of them. He had developed such deep friendships that wide receivers Cris Carter and Randy Moss took Larry under their wing and decided to teach him the game of football.

Several times a month, even after long, grueling football practices, Carter would take Larry aside and teach him personally how to be a wide receiver. He taught him how to run routes, catch footballs, avoid defenders, and increase speed. As you might expect, learning from the best paid off for Larry.

So much so that when Larry became a senior, Carter was quoted as saying, "This guy has more skills than any senior in high school I have ever seen." He went so far as to call his former college coaches and advise them to offer Larry a scholarship to play on their football team. Ultimately, Larry decided to attend the University of Pittsburgh to play for one of Carter's former coaches.

And now, two years later, Larry Fitzgerald was being selected by the Arizona Cardinals as the third player drafted in the 2004 draft. During only his first few years in the NFL, Fitzgerald would eventually go on to establish himself as one of the top wide receivers in the league— shattering many of the receiving records that had been established by Carter and Moss years earlier.[15] [16]

When I first saw the story on television, I reacted as any sports hero wannabe might react. I was jealous. I mean, how lucky is it that Larry Fitzgerald just happened to be in the right place to have that opportunity? He just happened to be invited by one of the greatest of all time to learn football? How could I not be jealous of someone that lucky?

But then it dawned on me. Wait a minute; I have been given that opportunity. Oh, I haven't been invited by a football superstar to learn football. I've been invited to something even better! I've been invited to live and learn from Jesus Christ himself.

Two thousand years ago, God became a man and walked on this very earth, inviting others to follow him. God created life. God loved life. And God desired that each person would be led into complete fullness and joy during life—both in the present and in the future. God's motives were entirely pure and for our benefit.

God's invitation to follow and learn from him is more than a "dream come true" that leads to worldly pleasures, status, accolades, or large paychecks. God's invitation is to find a life that fulfills the very destiny of our souls, hearts, and lives. It is, in fact, the very invitation we have been created to accept.

It involves every aspect of our lives: every decision, every action, every word, every dollar, every moment of our lives. And to miss the full scope of Christ's invitation is to miss out on the full life-giving relationship that leads to freedom, fulfillment, abundance, and glory. His invitation is the greatest that any of us could ever accept, and we would be wise to consider its weight. As soon as we begin to fully believe that truth, the words of Jesus sound less like life-draining commandments and more like life-giving invitations.

And suddenly, Christ's teachings on money and possessions begin to sound a bit different as well. His teachings to "sell your possessions and give to the poor" and to "not hoard up treasures here on earth" are not instructions designed to make my life miserable while on earth. They are not designed as some cosmic test of faith where I can prove if I really love him. They aren't given as some means of forcing sacrifice into my life.

They are an invitation—an invitation to live a more abundant life. And they should be considered the same way we consider Jesus' other teachings.

Why did Jesus tell us not to hate and kill? Because hating and killing eat you up inside. Why did Jesus tell us not to gossip? Because living as a gossip is a good way to lose friends. And why did Jesus tell us not to lie and cheat and steal? Because lying, cheating, and stealing are crummy ways to spend your days on earth. It's just not all that enjoyable in the long run. In other words, he was inviting us to a better way of life.

In the exact same way, why did Jesus invite us to sell our possessions, teach us to not hoard treasures on earth, and promise greater blessings to the poor? Because chasing and stockpiling possessions is an empty way to live life! It is a fruitless pursuit that wastes our time, our money, our energy, and our passion. And in the end, we have nothing to show for it because we can't take any of it with us.

But there is a better way! There is a quiet invitation that can only be heard by those who have the ears to hear it. There is an invitation to live with less. This unexpected key to happiness is available to anyone who refuses to measure wealth by the size of their home, the model of their car, or the brand names on their clothing. This newfound joy is available to anyone who chooses to reject the accumulation of excessive possessions. This abundant life is available to anyone who begins to finally believe that Jesus knew exactly what he was talking about when he encouraged us to give away possessions and pursue something greater instead.

Living with less is a key to happiness that perhaps nobody has ever given you—even though Jesus has been quietly inviting people to it for the last 2,000 years!

CHAPTER 10:
MAKING JESUS' STORY YOURS

How then do you make it a reality in your life? How do you begin living differently? How do you break the trend of consumerism— especially in a world that embraces it?

MAKE A CONSCIOUS DECISION TO PURSUE LIVING WITH LESS

Four years ago, we decided to begin living a minimalist life. At the time, the lifestyle of minimalism was completely foreign to us. It was entirely new. The thought of actually trying to live with fewer possessions had never been introduced to me. Yet it sounded surprisingly attractive. It resonated with something deep inside me. And my wife and I quickly embraced it. In fact, we started that very night by removing some of the items that we no longer used or loved.

Over the next few months and years, minimalism became a journey of experimentation, exploration, and trial and error. We were forced to identify our values— to clearly articulate what was most important to us. Ultimately, we found that living with less requires far more inspiration than instruction.

Minimalism—or whatever word you'd like to use when explaining the idea of living with less—is always going to look different from person to person and family to family. Our passions are different. Our personalities are different. Our pasts are different. Our present is different. As a result, the essentials of our lives are going to change. There is no checklist of things to own and things to throw away. The principles remain the same, but the specific actions of living with less will always look different.

We have all been told the exact same mistruths. We have all been tricked into thinking that the more we own, the happier we will be, the more joy we will experience, the more fulfilled we will be.

We've all been fed the same lies countless times since the day we were born. And only the truth about the joy of living with less can counteract that faulty premise.

As a result, the invitation to live with less is always going to require more inspiration than instruction. We must make a conscious decision to pursue it.

>>>**ACTION STEP:** *Decide today on these specific questions: "Do I see the benefit of living with fewer possessions? Will I commit my life to pursuing things of greater value than material possessions?"*

COUNT THE TRUE COST OF THE POSSESSIONS IN YOUR LIFE

With each purchase, we sign away a little piece of our lives. Most people view shopping as only a financial transaction. They see the price tag on an item and assume that is all the item will cost: $14.99 for a new T-shirt, $44.99 for a new video game, or $599 for a new iPad.

But the full cost of our purchases is never totaled at the cash register. The costs are only beginning.

T-shirts need to be washed... and dried... and folded... and picked up off the floor. Video games get played... and played... and played... and when they get beat (or boring), we buy new ones. Our iPads require cases... and apps... and data plans... and soon begin to call for our attention hours on end.

The full cost of our purchases is never displayed on tags in the department store. They only represent the initial cost. Their full cost always becomes far greater.

>>>**ACTION STEP:** *Before your next major purchase, ask yourself these questions: "Do I really need this item? What am I hoping it will accomplish in my life? What are the hidden costs associated with it—time, energy, expenses? Is there something more valuable I could purchase with my money instead?"*

BEGIN TO SEE MONEY DIFFERENTLY

The possession of money is not contrary to a minimalist life, but a minimalist life is not possible if money possesses you. The love of money can never be satisfied. You will never own enough. You will always desire more. And it keeps you, your attitude, and your actions in bondage.

When love of money is present, freedom is not. But money does not have to control your life. It does not have to dominate your ambition. You can be set free.

See money only as a tool to move through life. At its core, money is a bartering tool. It saves us from making our own clothes, tools, and furniture. Because of currency, I can spend my days doing what I love and am good at. In exchange, I receive money to trade with someone else who used their giftedness to create something different than me. That's it. That's the purpose. And if you have enough to meet your needs, you shouldn't commit the rest of your day to acquiring more.

With that as a foundation, we can learn to be content with poverty or great wealth. I have known poor people who live in complete contentment and I know rich people who are further from contentment today than when they were lacking. Your possessions do not lead to contentment. Your heart attitude does.

>>>**ACTION STEP:** *Track your spending for one month. How much money do you earn in one month (job, allowance, baby-sitting)? Now, track every purchase for one month: food, entertainment, shopping, gas, and everything else (you'll find this easier than it sounds). At the end of the month, you'll get a really good snapshot at how and where you spend your money. Ask yourself these follow-up questions: "Why did I spend my money the way that I did? What factors influenced my spending? Were they healthy, Christ-like reasons or something else?"*

UNDERSTAND THE SURROUNDING PRESSURE FROM OUR CULTURE

We recognize the culture of consumerism we're living in. We live in a culture that begs us to conform. Through its various messages, it calls us to squeeze into its mold. It exerts external pressure on our minds to believe in and buy its opinions, hopes, and aspirations. Yet the worldly pursuits that define most of our culture never satisfy our heart and soul.

In response, the world will tell us to run faster, reach further, work harder, make more, and become conformed more deeply. But its promised offer of fulfillment always remains out of reach. Our deepest longings are left unsatisfied.

Unfortunately, through this vicious cycle, we lose our uniqueness. We lose our passion. We lose our energy. We lose our opportunity to choose a different future. And because we are too busy chasing the wrong things, we sacrifice our opportunity to find something greater and more fulfilling in this life.

Meanwhile, our heart begs us to live differently. Our spirit calls us to seek our own passions. Our soul cries out for us to not conform. Our insides long for us to live countercultural lives. But all too often, the external pressure from the world calls us back into conformity. And we re-enter the race.

But it is time to become fully comfortable with the fact we have been called to something greater.

>>>ACTION STEP: *Clear the unnecessary clutter out of your bedroom. Look at each item specifically and ask yourself, "Do I really need this here?" If the answer is no, relocate it, recycle it, or discard it. As soon as you do, you'll understand exactly the feeling of freedom that accompanies owning less.*

REORIENT YOUR LIFE OFTEN AROUND THE OFFERINGS OF JESUS

The most valuable things in life cannot be seen with the naked eye: love, friendship, hope, integrity, trust, compassion.

These are the things that bring substance, fulfillment, and lasting joy to our lives. These are the things that Christ invites us to pursue.

But too often, we spend our time and energy chasing things that are visible: beautiful homes, fast cars, the latest technology, or more fashionable clothing. We dream of a future that includes those things. We plot and plan to acquire them. We go to great lengths to care for them, and we become jealous when others have more of them.

Yet those things have never brought us the fulfillment they promised. Instead, their appeal always dims, their value always decreases, their appearance always fades, and the satisfaction we receive from them diminishes every day.

It is time to shift our focus. It is time to allow the invisible to triumph in our eyes, minds, and hearts by offering the invisible room in our heart and mind. In Romans 12:2, Paul tells us that it is one thing to reject the patterns of this world, but we also need to be transformed into something else. Because our actions are almost always determined by our heart's desires and our mind's thoughts, it is absolutely essential for us to allow them to be transformed.

Bring the invisible into better focus. The old cliché is often true: "Out of sight, out of mind." Turn it around and use it to your advantage. Rather than spending so much energy soaking up television commercials, gift catalogs, fashion magazines, or window-shopping, find time to intentionally think about the eternal value found in the things of God. What images come into your mind when you think about joy, hope, faith, love, relationships, or significance? Take that image (or quote) and post it somewhere that you can see it to remind you of its value. This will help keep the invisible visible in your mind.

>>>ACTION STEP: *Test the teachings of Jesus in your life. Take some of your clothes (maybe even some that you still wear) and give them away. Spend some money on someone else* *this week. Donate an afternoon serving at a local charity you admire. When you do, you'll realize that happiness is found in serving others and that the things of God bring far more joy in the short and the long run.*

PURSUE THE GIFTS OF GOD WITH THE SAME PASSION YOU PURSUED THE WORLD

Be wise to culture's influence. Most of the Western world is built on humanity's desire to acquire more and more. It makes economies grow, causes governments to flourish, and brings appeasement to the masses. Therefore, it is encouraged at every turn. Become wise to these desires and learn to recognize their false promises.

Pursue the gifts of God with as much passion as you would the world's promises. In 1 Timothy 6:11, Paul writes to his young friend Timothy saying, *But you, man of God, flee from all this, and pursue righteousness, godliness, faith, love, endurance and gentleness.* How would our lives look different if we began pursuing the gifts of godliness, faith, and love with as much energy as we pursue new clothes, new electronics, and new cars? Not only would our lives improve immensely, but so would the world around us.

And it makes perfect sense. If the most valuable things in life are invisible, surely we should pursue them above everything else. After all, the rewards of righteousness, godliness, faith, love, endurance, and gentleness are far greater than anything the world may be offering.

>>>**ACTION STEP:** *Set aside one day to journal your thoughts. At the end of every hour, take a moment to reflect on where your mind wandered—write down anything you can remember thinking about. Although you'll never record everything you thought about, you'll likely notice a pattern forming. How much time was spent thinking on the things of God? How much time was spent thinking about worldly pursuits? If the balance doesn't seem right, create some reminders (quotes, photos, verses) that spur your mind toward the things of God.*

CHAPTER 11:

YOUR LIFE IS TOO VALUABLE TO SPEND CHASING POSSESSIONS

There is more joy in pursuing less than can be found in pursuing more. As I mentioned before, this is a message that we already know to be true.

It's just that since the day we were born, we have been told something different. We have been told that possessions equal joy. And because we have heard that message so many times and from so many angles, we have begun to believe it. As a result, we spend our lives working long hours to make good money so we can buy nice stuff.

But when we again hear the simple message that there is more joy in pursuing less, it rings true in our hearts. Because deep down, we know it to be true. We know possessions don't equal joy. And we know our life is far too valuable to waste chasing them.

It just helps to be reminded from time to time. As you go forward with the rest of your life, remember...

Our lives are short. We only get one shot at it. The time goes by quickly. And once we use it up, we can't get it back. So make the most of it. Possessions steal our time and energy. They require unending maintenance to be cleaned, maintained, fixed, replaced, and removed. They steal our precious attention, time, and energy, and we don't even notice it—until it's too late.

Our lives are unique. Our look, our personality, our talents, and the people who have influenced our lives have made us special. As a result, our lives are exactly like no one else. And just because everyone else is chasing material possessions doesn't mean we have to, too.

Our lives are significant. Far more than success, our hearts desire significance. Significance lasts forever; possessions are temporal. They perish, spoil, and fade. And most of them are designed to break so you'll fix or replace them. Significance will always outlast you. Even when you are no longer present, your significance will still be yours. And nothing can ever take that away from you.

Our lives are designed to inspire. Make footprints worth following. Nobody ever changed the world by mimicking someone else. Instead, people who change the world live differently and inspire others to do the same. Possessions may briefly impress, but they never inspire. God-honoring lives do.

Our lives are important. Our heart and soul make us valuable. Don't sacrifice your important role in this world by settling for possessions that can be purchased with a card of plastic.

Our lives deserve better. Joy, happiness, and fulfillment are found in the invisible things of life: love, hope, peace, and relationships. They are not for sale at your local department store. Stop looking for them there. People who live their lives in the pursuit of possessions are never content. They always desire what's newer, faster, or bigger because material possessions can never satisfy our deepest heart desires.

Your life is far too valuable to waste chasing material possessions. Find more joy today and throughout the rest of your life by choosing to pursue "greater," rather than "more." Imagine what you could accomplish with your life if you chose to live with fewer possessions.

Because that's what Jesus has been offering all along...

ENDNOTES

1. *The Survey of Consumer Payment Choice* (Boston, MA: Federal Reserve Bank of Boston, January 2010), 53.

2. Calculated by dividing the total revolving debt in the U.S. ($801 billion as of December 2011 data, as listed in the Federal Reserve's February 2012 report on consumer credit) by the estimated number of households carrying credit card debt (50.2 million).

3. Robert Weagley, "One Big Difference Between Chinese and American Households: Debt," Forbes (June 24, 2010); accessible at forbes.com/sites/moneybuilder/2010/06/24/one-big-difference-between-chinese-and-american-households-debt. Retrieved May 7, 2012.

4. Paul Lukas, "Our Malls. Ourselves," Fortune Magazine via CNN Money (October 18, 2004); accessible at money.cnn.com/magazines/fortune/fortune_archive/2004/10/18/8188067/index.htm. Retrieved May 7, 2012.

5. "Women Spend Eight Years of their Life Shopping," Daily Mail Online (November 27, 2006); accessible at dailymail.co.uk/femail/article-419077/Women-spend-years-life-shopping.html. Retrieved May 7, 2012.

6. Jon Mooallem. "The Self-Storage Self," The New York Times (September 2, 2009); accessible at nytimes.com/2009/09/06/magazine/06self-storage-t.html. Retrieved May 7, 2012.

7. Naomi Seldin Ramirez. "America's Clutter Problem Fueled Self-Storage Industry," Albany Times Union (September 8, 2009); accessible at blog.timesunion.com/simplerliving/date/2009/page/18. Retrieved May 7, 2012.

8. *2010 Television Audience Report from Nielsen* (New York, NY: A.C. Nielsen Co., December 2011), 5.

9. "Quotable Quotes," Reader's Digest (March 2006), 81.

10. Caitlin A. Johnson, "Cutting Through Advertising Clutter," CBS News (February 11, 2009); accessible at cbsnews.com/2100-3445_162-2015684.html. Retrieved May 7, 2012

11. Ramirez, "America's Clutter Problem Fueled Self-Storage Industry."

12. "The Average American Consumer: Over 30 Percent of Income Spent on Housing," U.S. News and World Report (July 13, 2009); accessible at usnews.com/opinion/articles/2009/07/13/the-average-american-consumer-over-30-percent-of-income-spent-on-housing. Retrieved on May 7, 2012.

13. John Ruskin, *The Works of John Ruskin: Volume IV; The Eagle's Nest* (London, England: Smith, Elder, and Co., 1872), 86.

14. Samuel Alexander and Simon Ussher, *Voluntary Simplicity Movement Report: A Multi-National Survey Analysis in Theoretical Context* (Melbourne, Australia: Simplicity Institute, 2011), 10.

15. "Larry Fitzgerald: Ballboy. An Interview with Cris Carter." ESPN SportsCenter. Originally aired on January 21, 2009. Accessible at blinkx.com/watch-video/larry-fitzgerald-talks-about-being-a-ball-boy-for-cris-carter/cbueiTStx8NNE2WabgVP8Q.

16. "Larry Fitzgerald," Pop Warner Football Online; accessible at popwarner.com/scholastics/2005/larryfitzgerald.asp. Retrieved May 7, 2012.